POPE BENEDICT XVI

THE PRIESTHOOD

Spiritual Thoughts Series

Preface by Cardinal Séan O'Malley
Introduction by Lucio Coco and
Edmund Caruana, OCarm

United States Conference of Catholic Bishops
Washington, D.C.

OTHER TITLES IN THE SPIRITUAL THOUGHTS SERIES

Cover photo, *L'Osservatore Romano*

First printing, July 2009

ISBN: 978-1-60137-086-0

CONTENTS

od *is the only wealth that people want to find in a priest.*

Pope Benedict XVI

PREFACE

he primary association of the priesthood, both in the consciousness of the Christian people and in the self-understanding of the priest himself, is with the Eucharist. It is here that all other tasks find their unity; in the Eucharist we are joined to Christ and to all other communities. We name the pope and the bishop in the eucharistic prayer to express the fellowship we have with the entire Church. When the priest pronounces the words "This is my body," he speaks them *in persona Christi*, in the person of Christ. It is a call to dedicate our very existence to God. A priest's existence must be wholly dedicated to God and to others; he must become a sacrificial gift.

The people know that the priest is a man of God; this is why they open their homes to him. They tell the priest their hopes and their fears, their joys and their sins. They speak to him in the hope that, by opening their hearts to him, they have opened their hearts to God. One of the greatest joys of the priesthood is to be able to tell people of God's abundant mercy and to assure them that our God is always ready, even anxious, to forgive us. Jesus does not only proclaim the forgiveness of God the Father; Jesus himself forgives, saying many times: "Your sins are forgiven." Jesus grants this same power to his priests: "Receive the Holy Spirit. Whose sins you forgive are forgiven them" (Jn 20:22-23).

There are many trials and struggles of our priestly lives, difficulties that come from life itself and difficulties that arise from our own broken humanity. But these are nothing compared to the majesty of our calling: the priest is friend to all that is holy and of God, called to live his life with integrity and peace.

We must be attentive to the missionary aspect of our priestly identity: we are sent to proclaim the Good News to the poor, and especially to those who are impoverished by being far from the Gospel and the community of faith. The missionary urgency of the present time in our Church demands a renewal of pastoral practice and bold strategies that addresses the new challenges of our Church today. We need a new apologetic to respond to the questions that contemporary people have. Our catechetical efforts must be about mentoring people in the faith in a worshiping community. We need to instill in our people a sense of vocation, a generous response to God's call to serve and to sacrifice in a particular way of life, especially married life, family life, and the priesthood.

Our task is to introduce Christ to the multitudes who do not yet know, or who have forgotten, that he is alive and he loves them and he acts through his Body, the Church. We pray that Mary, the Mother of the Good Shepherd, will help us to be priests after her Son's own Heart.

Cardinal Seán O'Malley
Archbishop of Boston
July 2009

Introduction

or the occasion of the Year for Priests beginning on June 19, 2009, and ending on June 19, 2010, which was declared in honor of Saint John Vianney on the 150th anniversary of the death of the Holy Curé d'Ars, this volume of the Spiritual Thoughts Series on the thoughts of Benedict XVI gathers the reflections of the Holy Father on the topic of priesthood. The starting date of this initiative coincides with the Solemnity of the Sacred Heart of Jesus, which is the day on which the Church celebrates World Day for the Sanctification of Priests. It is Pope Benedict himself who explains the meaning of this term: sanctification is "the giving over of a person to God" (Homily, April 9, 2009). This consecration also defines the essence of the priesthood: "it is a transfer of ownership, a being taken out of the world and given to God" (Homily, April 9, 2009). While removing him from the world, this type of sacrifice—which separates a person from ordinary life and consigns him to God (see Address, August 8, 2008)—places the consecrated man in a situation of intimacy with God, in a relationship and in dialogue with him, which is a necessary condition for enabling the priest to bring God into the world, for enabling him to respond to the people's thirst for God and to the "need to be reminded of the ultimate purpose of their lives" (Address, April 16, 2008), thereby becoming a visible sign of God's presence. "This is the central task of the priest: to bring God to men and women. Of course, he can only do this if he himself comes from God, if he lives *with* and *by* God" (Address, December 22, 2006).

The relationship of the priest with God, remaining in his truth, binds him to the Truth who is Christ (see Jn 14:6). Through this sacrament he is brought into Christ: he enters into relation with the Father through the Son, and through a deepening of this bond, he therefore becomes capable of revealing the nature of this God to the world: not an enigmatic and terrible God, but "a God with a human face, a God who is love" (Address, March 2, 2006). In virtue of the sacrament, he is able to enter into contact with the person of Christ and to speak and act in his name, representing to the world this power of love through which the priesthood of Christ finds expression. Since he carries out his ministry *in persona Christi* (in the person of Christ), the priest continues the saving actions of Christ, "breaking the Bread of life and remitting sins" (Homily, May 3, 2009), through which he has been granted the power to reintegrate man into the very heart of God and to offer him the possibility of redemption and forgiveness. As an *alter Christus* (other Christ), the sacrifice that the priest celebrates and the absolution he gives are grounded on this Otherness that passes through him, by means of the sacrament, and makes him "a humble instrument pointing to Christ, who offers himself in sacrifice for the salvation of the world" (Address, March 18, 2009).

It is within this mystery, which binds the priest to God, sanctifying him and consecrating him in truth, immersing him in and uniting him to Christ, that the priest cultivates a prayerful spirituality in order to "spend time in God's presence" (Address, May 13, 2005) and to "'remain' in Christ" (Homily, May 3, 2009; see Jn 1:35-39, 15:4-10). The Holy Father continually calls to mind this prayerful dimension through which the priest builds his conversation with God and lives the encounter with Christ, and he also offers a reminder of the various forms of prayer available to a priest for nurturing his spiritual life. First and foremost, the Eucharistic celebration "is the greatest and highest act of prayer" (Homily, May 3, 2009) and constitutes the core from which all other forms of prayer radiate: the Liturgy of the Hours, the Divine Office, eucharistic adoration, the holy Rosary, and meditation, which "fulfill the words of Jesus in the priest's day and in all his life" (Homily, May 3, 2009).

The "sacredness" to which consecration destines the priest and in which the life of prayer sustains him is not equivalent, of course, to segregation and exclusion from the world. As the Holy Father explains, "'extraction from the common' means 'consignment to the whole'" (Address, August 6, 2008), and it is an important way of serving one's brothers and sisters and of being available to everyone, starting with God (see Homily, April 9, 2009). His ministry is totally dependent on this relationship that makes him fully available to others through first making himself available to the Lord in the fullness of his being (see Address, August 6, 2008). It is in this full availability to the Lord, as the expression of this totality, that his service to others, his work, and his pastoral care find their purpose. This making oneself "all things to all," as Saint Paul says (see 1 Cor 9:22), is therefore the characteristic of every priest and finds its most evident expression "in daily life, in attention to every person and family" (Address, May 13, 2005), which gives life to his mission and continually moves him toward other people in order to bring the focus back to "attention to the choice of God . . . and also to teach friendship with Jesus Christ" (Address, February 7, 2008).

These are a few of the reflection points that can be drawn from the Holy Father's words to priests from frequent homilies and meetings with the clergy of the Italian dioceses and of the world on the occasions of pastoral visits and apostolic trips. He steadfastly entreats them in order to accompany and support them in carrying out a mandate that is not always simple and easy in a world that "does not want to know God . . . and . . . does not want to listen to his ministers" (Homily, May 3, 2009)—but a mandate that constitutes the most necessary and engaging adventure for the world: "the adventure of showing, of making present, the fullness of life to which we all aspire" (Homily, February 1, 2008).

Lucio Coco

Edmondo Caruana, OCarm

THE
PRIESTHOOD

riests will put nothing before love of Christ.

—POPE BENEDICT XVI
ANGELUS, JUNE 5, 2005

I. THE FRIEND OF JESUS

1. *Program*

[Dear brother priests], may Christ who is the Way, the Truth and the Life (cf. Jn 14:6), be the object of our thought, the topic of our words, the reason for our life.

> *Meeting with priests in the Cathedral of Brindisi*
> *June 15, 2008*

2. *Friend of Jesus*

Being a priest means becoming an ever closer friend of Jesus Christ with the whole of our existence.

> *Homily at Chrism Mass, Holy Thursday*
> *April 13, 2006*

3. *Need*

The world needs God—not just any god but the God of Jesus Christ, the God who made himself flesh and blood, who loved us to the point of dying for us, who rose and created within himself room for man. This God must live in us and we in him. This is our priestly call: only in this way can our action as priests bear fruit.

Homily at Chrism Mass, Holy Thursday
April 13, 2006

4. *In the name of Jesus*

The priest receives his "name," his very identity, from Christ. Everything he does is done in his name. His "I" becomes totally relative to the "I" of Jesus.

Homily at Mass for the ordination of priests
May 3, 2009

5. *In the light of God*

First of all, in our hearts we [priests] must live the relationship with Christ and, through him, with the Father; only then can we truly understand people, only in the light of God can the depths of man be understood. Then those who are listening to us realize that we are not speaking of ourselves or of some thing, but of the true Shepherd.

Homily at Mass for the ordination of priests
May 7, 2006

6. *To choose life*

This is our priestly vocation: to choose life ourselves and to help others to choose life. . . . to help people make the true choice for life, to renew their relationship with God as the relationship which gives us life and shows us the way to life. And thus, to love Christ anew, who from being the most unknown Being whom we did not reach and who remained enigmatic, became a known God, a God with a human face, a God who is love.

> *Meeting with clergy of the Diocese of Rome*
> *March 2, 2006*

7. *Friendship of Christ*

The first imperative [of a priest] is to be a man of God, in the sense of a man in friendship with Christ and with his Saints.

> *Meeting with clergy of the Dioceses of*
> *Belluno-Feltre and Treviso*
> *July 24, 2007*

8. *Root*

Dear priests, the quality of your lives and your pastoral service seem to indicate that in this Diocese, as in many others of the world, we have now left behind us that period of identity crisis that troubled so many priests. However, still present are the causes of the "spiritual wilderness" that afflict humanity in our day and consequently also undermine the Church, which dwells among humankind. How can we not fear that they may also ensnare the lives of priests? It is indispensable, therefore, to return ever anew to the solid root of our priesthood. This root, as we well know, is one: Jesus Christ our Lord.

Address to clergy of the Diocese of Rome
May 13, 2005

9. *Friend of Jesus*

Dear priests . . . the Lord calls us friends, he makes us his friends, he entrusts himself to us, he entrusts to us his Body in the Eucharist, he entrusts to us his Church. Therefore, we must be true friends to him, we must have the same perception as he has, we must want what he wants and not what he does not want. Jesus himself tells us: "You are my friends if you do what I command you" (Jn 15:14). Let this be our common resolution: all of us together, to do his holy will, in which lies our freedom and our joy.

Address to clergy of the Diocese of Rome
May 13, 2005

10. *Relationship*

Since the priesthood is rooted in Christ, it is by its nature in the Church and for the Church. Indeed, the Christian faith is not something purely spiritual and internal, nor is our relationship with Christ itself exclusively subjective and private. Rather, it is a completely concrete and ecclesial relationship.

Address to clergy of the Diocese of Rome
May 13, 2005

II. Consecrated in Truth

11. *Consecration*

[The priesthood] is a transfer of ownership, a being taken out of the world and given to God.

> *Homily at Chrism Mass, Holy Thursday*
> *April 9, 2009*

12. *Ordination*

The Sacrament of Ordination expresses this very point: through the Sacrament the priest is totally inserted into Christ, so that by starting from him and acting in his sight he may carry out in communion with him the service of Jesus, the one Shepherd, in whom God, as man, wants to be our Shepherd.

> *Homily at Mass for the ordination of priests*
> *May 7, 2006*

13. *Sign*

The priest, for the Church and in the Church, is a humble but real sign of the one, eternal Priest who is Jesus. He must proclaim his word authoritatively, renew his acts of pardon and offering and exercise loving concern in the service of his flock, in communion with the Pastors and faithfully docile to the teaching of the Magisterium.

Meeting with priests, seminarians, and
students in Sardinia, Italy
September 7, 2008

14. In persona Christi

The mystery of the priesthood of the Church lies in the fact that we, miserable human beings, by virtue of the Sacrament, can speak with [the] "*I*" [of Jesus]: *in persona Christi*. He wishes to exercise *his* priesthood through us.

Homily at Chrism Mass, Holy Thursday
April 13, 2006

15. *In the name of Christ*

Believe in the power of your priesthood! By virtue of the sacrament, you have received all that you are. When you utter the words "I" and "my" ("I absolve you . . . This is my body . . ."), you do it not in your own name, but in the name of Christ, "*in persona Christi*," who wants to use your lips and your hands, your spirit of sacrifice and your talent.

Meeting with clergy in Warsaw, Poland
May 25, 2006

16. *Consecrated in truth*

To become priests in the Church means to enter into this self-donation of Christ through the Sacrament of Orders and to enter with all of one's being. Jesus gave his life for all, but in a special way he consecrated himself for those the Father had given to him, that they may be consecrated in truth, that is in him, and could speak and act in his name, represent him, continue his saving actions: breaking the Bread of life and remitting sins.

Homily at Mass for the ordination of priests
May 3, 2009

17. *Bring God*

This is the central task of the priest: to bring God to men and women. Of course, he can only do this if he himself comes from God, if he lives *with* and *by* God.

Christmas address to the Roman Curia
December 22, 2006

18. *Coherence*

Our being priests is simply a new and radical way of being united to Christ. In its substance, it has been bestowed on us for ever in the sacrament. But this new seal imprinted upon our being can become for us a condemnation, if our lives do not develop by entering into the truth of the Sacrament.

Homily at Chrism Mass, Holy Thursday
April 9, 2009

19. *Immersion*

Priestly ordination means: being immersed in him, immersed in the Truth. I belong in a new way to him and thus to others, "that his Kingdom may come."

Homily at Chrism Mass, Holy Thursday
April 9, 2009

20. *Discipleship and service*

One enters the priesthood through the Sacrament, and this means precisely: through the gift of oneself to Christ, so that he can make use of me; so that I may serve him and follow his call, even if it proves contrary to my desire for self-fulfillment and esteem.

Homily at Mass for the ordination of priests
May 7, 2006

21. *To ordinands*

The Sacrament of Orders, which you are about to receive, will make you sharers in the very mission of Christ; you will be called to scatter the seed of his Word, the seed that carries in itself the Kingdom of God; to dispense divine mercy and to nourish the faithful at the table of his Body and Blood.

Homily at Mass for the ordination of
priests for the Diocese of Rome
April 29, 2007

22. *Necessity*

There will always be a need for the priest who is totally dedicated to the Lord and therefore totally dedicated to humanity. . . . On the one hand . . . we are consigned to the Lord, separated from ordinary life, but on the other, we are consigned to him because in this way we can belong to him totally and totally belong to others.

Meeting with clergy of the
Diocese of Bolzano-Bressanone
August 6, 2008

23. *Celibacy*

[The priest must] make [himself] available to the Lord in the fullness of [his] being and consequently [find himself] totally available to men and women. I think celibacy is a fundamental expression of this totality and already, for this reason, an important reference in this world because it only has meaning if we truly believe in eternal life and if we believe that God involves us and that we can be for him.

Meeting with clergy of the
Diocese of Bolzano-Bressanone
August 6, 2008

III. The Sacramental Dimension

24. *Exchange*

In priesthood there is an exchange: in the administration of the sacraments, the priest now acts and speaks "*in persona Christi.*" In the sacred mysteries, he does not represent himself and does not speak expressing himself, but speaks for the Other, for Christ.

> *Homily at Chrism Mass, Holy Thursday*
> *April 5, 2007*

Eucharistic Centrality

25. *Eucharist and the Sacrament of Orders*

By virtue of sacred Orders, the priest receives the gift of and commitment to repeating in the Sacrament the gestures and words with which Jesus instituted the memorial of his Pasch at the Last Supper. This great miracle of love, which the priest is called ever more faithfully to witness and proclaim (cf. Apostolic Letter *Mane Nobiscum Domine*, no. 30), is renewed in his hands. This is the reason why the priest must be first and foremost an adorer who contemplates the Eucharist, starting from the very moment in which he celebrates it. We are well aware that the validity of the Sacrament does not depend on the holiness of the celebrant, but its effectiveness for him and for others will be all the greater the deeper the faith, the more ardent the love and the more fervent the spirit of prayer with which he lives it.

Angelus
September 18, 2005

26. "Adoro te devote, latens Deitas" ["I devoutly adore you, hidden God"]

We priests of the New Covenant . . . are every day witnesses and ministers of the "epiphany" of Jesus Christ in the Holy Eucharist. The Church celebrates all the mysteries of the Lord in this most holy and most humble Sacrament in which he both reveals and conceals his glory. "*Adoro te devote, latens Deitas*" in adoration, thus we pray along with Saint Thomas Aquinas.

> *Homily on the Feast of the Epiphany*
> *January 6, 2009*

27. *Encounter*

The Holy Eucharist, in which the sacrifice of Jesus on the Cross remains continually present, truly present among us, is rightly at the center of priestly life. And with this as our starting point, we also learn what celebrating the Eucharist properly means: it is an encounter with the Lord, who strips himself of his divine glory for our sake, allows himself to be humiliated to the point of death on the Cross and thus gives himself to each one of us.

> *Homily at Mass for the ordination of priests*
> *May 7, 2006*

28. Amoris officium [office of love]

At times, the ministerial priesthood has a constitutive relationship with the Body of Christ in his dual and inseparable dimensions as Eucharist and as Church, as Eucharistic body and Ecclesial body. Therefore, our ministry is *amoris officium* (Saint Augustine, *In Iohannis Evangelium Tractatus* 123, 5), it is the office of the Good Shepherd who offers his life for his sheep (cf. Jn 10:14-15). In the Eucharistic mystery, Christ gives himself ever anew, and it is precisely in the Eucharist that we learn love of Christ, hence, love for the Church.

Address to clergy of the Diocese of Rome
May 13, 2005

29. *Eucharistic love*

Whoever places himself at the service of the Gospel, if he lives the Eucharist, makes progress in love of God and neighbor and thus contributes to building the Church as communion. We can affirm that the "Eucharistic love" motivates and founds the vocational activity of the whole Church, because, as I wrote in the Encyclical *God Is Love* (*Deus Caritas Est*), vocations to the priesthood and to other ministries and services flourish within the people of God wherever there are those in whom Christ can be seen through his Word, in the sacraments and especially in the Eucharist.

Message for the Forty-Fourth World Day of Vocations
February 10, 2007

30. *The Eucharistic celebration*

The ministerial priesthood entails a profound relationship with Christ who is given to us in the Eucharist. Let the celebration of the Eucharist be truly the center of your priestly lives; in this way it will also be the center of your ecclesial mission. Throughout our lives Christ calls us to share in his mission, to be his witnesses, so that his word may be proclaimed to all. In celebrating this sacrament in the Lord's name and in his person, the person of the priest cannot occupy center stage; he is a servant, a humble instrument pointing to Christ, who offers himself in sacrifice for the salvation of the world.

Homily at Vespers with clergy in Yaoundé, Cameroon
March 18, 2009

31. *School of life*

Priests, like every baptized person, live by Eucharistic communion with the Lord. It is impossible to receive the Lord every day, taking his Body and Blood into our hands, pronouncing the tremendous and wonderful words: "This is my Body, this is my Blood" without letting ourselves be seized by him, without letting ourselves be won over by fascination for him, without letting his infinite love change us from within. May the Eucharist become a school of life for you [priests] in which Jesus' sacrifice on the Cross teaches you to make a total gift of yourselves to your brethren.

Address to the community of the
Pontifical Ecclesiastical Academy
June 9, 2008

32. *Eucharistic mystery*

The daily Eucharist is very important for the priest. In it he exposes himself ever anew to this mystery; ever anew he puts himself in God's hands, experiencing at the same time the joy of knowing that He is present, receives me, ever anew raises and supports me, gives me his hand, himself. The Eucharist must become for us a school of life in which we learn to give our lives.

Homily at Mass for the ordination of priests
May 7, 2006

Reconciliation and the Other Sacraments

33. *The ministry of reconciliation*

Jesus Christ was sent by the Father, through the power of the Holy Spirit, for the salvation of the entire human family, and we priests are enabled through the grace of the sacrament to share in this mission of his. As the Apostle Paul writes, "God . . . has given us the ministry of reconciliation. . . . This makes us ambassadors for Christ, God as it were appealing through us. We implore you, in Christ's name: be reconciled to God" (2 Cor 5:18-29). This is how Saint Paul describes our mission as priests.

Address to clergy of the Diocese of Rome
May 13, 2005

34. *The sacrament of forgiveness*

Lastly, there is the [priest's] power of forgiveness. The Sacrament of Penance is one of the Church's precious treasures, since authentic world renewal is accomplished only through forgiveness. Nothing can improve the world if evil is not overcome. Evil can be overcome only by forgiveness. Certainly, it must be an effective forgiveness; but only the Lord can give us this forgiveness, a forgiveness that drives away evil not only with words but truly destroys it. Only suffering can bring this about and it has truly taken place with the suffering love of Christ, from whom we draw the power to forgive.

> *Homily at Pentecost Mass for priestly ordinations*
> *May 15, 2005*

35. *The cure of souls*

The ministry of Reconciliation is an act of extraordinary caring which the person needs in order to be perfectly healthy. Thus, this sacramental care begins with Baptism, which is the fundamental renewal of our life, and extends to the Sacrament of Reconciliation and the Anointing of the Sick. Of course, all the other sacraments and also the Eucharist involve great care for souls. We have to care for people but above all—this is our mandate [as priests]—for their souls.

Meeting with clergy of the Dioceses of
Belluno-Feltre and Treviso
July 24, 2007

36. *Sacrament*

Therefore, the priesthood is indispensable because in the Eucharist itself, originating in God, the Church is built; in the Sacrament of Penance purification is conferred; in the Sacrament, the priesthood is, precisely, an involvement in the "for" of Jesus Christ.

Meeting with clergy of the
Diocese of Bolzano-Bressanone
August 6, 2008

IV. THE
SPIRITUAL LIFE

Spiritual Paternity

37. *Priestly spirituality*

The priest . . . should make his spiritual life his highest
priority. He is called to seek God tirelessly, while remaining
attuned to the concerns of his brothers and sisters.

> *Apostolic Exhortation* The Sacrament of Charity
> [Sacramentum Caritatis], *no. 80*
> *February 22, 2007*

38. *Specialists*

The faithful expect only one thing from priests: that they
be specialists in promoting the encounter between man and
God. The priest is not asked to be an expert in economics,
construction or politics. He is expected to be an expert in
the spiritual life.

> *Meeting with clergy in Warsaw, Poland*
> *May 25, 2006*

39. *Spiritual paternity*

Christ needs priests who are mature, virile, capable of cultivating an authentic spiritual paternity. For this to happen, priests need to be honest with themselves, open with their spiritual director and trusting in divine mercy.

> *Meeting with clergy in Warsaw, Poland*
> *May 25, 2006*

40. *Spiritual act*

Being a pastor is in itself a spiritual act. . . . This means that he himself lives first of all on the Word of God.

> *Meeting with clergy of the Diocese of Rome*
> *February 22, 2007*

41. *Priestly ascesis*

The art of priestly ascesis which is also necessary today . . . should not be exercised on a par with pastoral activities as an additional burden that makes our day even more difficult. On the contrary, we must learn how to surpass ourselves, how to give and how to offer our lives.

> *Address to clergy of the Diocese of Rome*
> *May 13, 2005*

42. *Consolation*

In existing "for others," I am in the Crucified and Risen Lord. I think this is a great consolation for parish priests and Bishops. Even if little time is left for contemplation, in being "for others," we are with the Lord.

Meeting with clergy of the Diocese of Rome
February 22, 2007

The Virtue of the Priest

43. *Orientation*

I believe the most important thing is, first of all, that the life [of priests] should be oriented to the Holy Spirit, because we live in the milieu of the Spirit, in the body of Christ, and from this we experience humanization, we nurture the simple human virtues and thus learn to be good in the broadest sense of the word. Thus, one acquires a sensitivity for good initiatives which later, of course, develop a missionary force and in a certain sense prepare the ground for the moment when it becomes reasonable and comprehensible to speak of Christ and of our faith.

Meeting with clergy of the
Diocese of Bolzano-Bressanone
August 6, 2008

44. *Exhortation*

[Priests], be authentic in your life and your ministry. Gazing upon Christ, live a modest life, in solidarity with the faithful to whom you have been sent. Serve everyone; be accessible in the parishes and in the confessionals, accompany the new movements and associations, support families, do not forget the link with young people, remember the poor and the abandoned. If you live by faith, the Holy Spirit will suggest to you what you must say and how you must serve.

Meeting with clergy in Warsaw, Poland
May 25, 2006

45. *Portrait*

[The priest] is a man of prayer, a man of forgiveness, a man who receives and celebrates the sacraments as acts of prayer and encounter with the Lord. He is a man of charity, lived and practiced, thus all the simple acts, conversation, encounter, everything that needs to be done, become spiritual acts in communion with Christ.

Meeting with clergy of the Diocese of Rome
February 22, 2007

46. *Renunciation*

In the words "I do," spoken at our priestly ordination, we made this fundamental renunciation of our desire to be independent, "self-made." But day by day this great "yes" has to be lived out in the many little "yeses" and small sacrifices. This "yes" made up of tiny steps which together make up the great "yes" can be lived out without bitterness and self-pity only if Christ is truly the center of our lives. If we enter into true closeness to him.

> *Homily at Chrism Mass, Holy Thursday*
> *April 9, 2009*

47. *Ascent*

The only legitimate ascent towards the shepherd's ministry is the Cross. This is the true way to rise; this is the true door. It is not the desire to become "someone" for oneself, but rather to exist for others, for Christ, and thus through him and with him to be there for the people he seeks, whom he wants to lead on the path of life.

> *Homily at Mass for the ordination of priests*
> *May 7, 2006*

48. Diakonéin

Every priest, of course, also continues to be a deacon and must always be aware of this dimension, for the Lord himself became our minister, our deacon. Recall the act of the washing of the feet, where it is explicitly shown that the Teacher, the Lord, acts as a deacon and wants those who follow him to be deacons and carry out this ministry for humanity, to the point that they even help us to wash the dirty feet of the people entrusted to our care. This dimension seems to me to be of paramount importance.

Meeting with clergy of the Diocese of Rome
February 7, 2008

49. *Mandate*

This is . . . the true nature of our priesthood. In fact, all that constitutes our priestly ministry cannot be the product of our personal abilities. This is true for the administration of the Sacraments, but it is also true for the service of the Word: we are not sent to proclaim ourselves or our personal opinions, but the mystery of Christ and, in him, the measure of true humanism.

Address to clergy of the Diocese of Rome
May 13, 2005

50. *Sign*

The priest, for the Church and in the Church, is a humble but real sign of the one, eternal Priest who is Jesus. He must proclaim his word authoritatively, renew his acts of pardon and offering and exercise loving concern in the service of his flock, in communion with the Pastors and faithfully docile to the teaching of the Magisterium.

> *Meeting with priests, seminarians, and*
> *students in Sardinia, Italy*
> *September 7, 2008*

51. *Poverty*

For us priests . . . the issue of poverty and the poor must be the object of a constant and serious examination of conscience. In our own situation, in which we are not badly off, we are not poor, I think that we ought to reflect particularly on how we can live out this calling in a sincere way. I would like to recommend it for your—for our—examination of conscience.

> *Homily at Vespers with clergy and*
> *religious at Mariazell, Austria*
> *September 8, 2007*

52. *Chastity*

Priests and religious are not aloof from interpersonal relationships. Chastity, on the contrary, means . . . an intense relationship; it is, positively speaking, a relationship with the living Christ and, on the basis of that, with the Father. Consequently, by the vow of celibate chastity we do not consecrate ourselves to individualism or a life of isolation; instead, we solemnly promise to put completely and unreservedly at the service of God's Kingdom—and thus at the service of others—the deep relationships of which we are capable and which we receive as a gift.

Homily at Vespers with clergy and
religious at Mariazell, Austria
September 8, 2007

53. *Obedience*

Listening to God and obeying him has nothing to do with external constraint and the loss of oneself. Only by entering into God's will do we attain our true identity. Our world today needs the testimony of this experience precisely because of its desire for "self-realization" and "self-determination."

Homily at Vespers with clergy and
religious at Mariazell, Austria
September 8, 2007

54. *Secret*

Holiness is the secret of the true success of your priestly ministry.

Homily at Vespers in the Roman Major Seminary
February 1, 2008

Time for Prayer

55. *Remain in Christ*

We priests derive a particular vocation to pray in a strongly Christocentric sense: we are called, that is, to "remain" in Christ as the evangelist John likes to repeat (cf. Jn 1:35-39; 15:4-10) and this abiding in Christ is achieved especially through prayer. Our ministry is totally tied to this "abiding" which is equivalent to prayer, and draws from this its efficacy.

> *Homily at Mass for the ordination of priests*
> *May 3, 2009*

56. *Man of prayer*

The priest must above all be a man of prayer. The world in its frenetic activism often loses its direction. Its action and capacities become destructive if they lack the power of prayer, from which flow the waters of life that irrigate the arid land.

> *Homily at Chrism Mass, Holy Thursday*
> *April 13, 2006*

57. *Requirement*

The prayer of a priest is a requirement of his pastoral ministry. This is because no community can forego the witness of a prayerful priest who proclaims transcendence and is immersed in God's mystery.

Address to bishops from Mexico on their ad limina *visit*
September 23, 2005

58. *Priestly reading*

Dear brother priests, do not be afraid to spend much time reading and meditating on the Scriptures and praying the Divine Office! Almost without your knowing it, God's word, read and pondered in the Church, acts upon you and transforms you. As the manifestation of divine Wisdom, if that word becomes your life "companion," it will be your "good counselor" and an "encouragement in cares and grief" (Wis 8:9).

Homily at Vespers with clergy and
religious in Lourdes, France
September 12, 2008

59. Having time

A fundamental priority of priestly life is to be with the Lord and thus to have time for prayer.

Meeting with clergy of the
Diocese of Bolzano-Bressanone
August 6, 2008

60. The service of prayer

The time he spends in prayer is the most important time in a priest's life, in which divine grace acts with greater effectiveness, making his ministry fruitful. The first service to render to the community is prayer.

Meeting with priests in the Cathedral of Brindisi
June 15, 2008

61. The fruits of prayer

Let us not be consumed with haste, as if time dedicated to Christ in silent prayer were time wasted. On the contrary, it is precisely then that the most wonderful fruits of pastoral service come to birth. There is no need to be discouraged on account of the fact that prayer requires effort, or because of the impression that Jesus remains silent. He is indeed silent, but he is at work.

Meeting with clergy in Warsaw, Poland
May 25, 2006

62. *Priority*

Spending time in God's presence in prayer is a real pastoral priority; it is not an addition to pastoral work: being before the Lord is a pastoral priority and in the final analysis, the most important.

Address to clergy of the Diocese of Rome
May 13, 2005

63. *Forms of prayer*

[The prayer of a priest has different forms], first of all [the] daily Holy Mass. The Eucharistic Celebration is the greatest and highest act of prayer, and constitutes the center and the source from which even the other forms receive "nourishment": the Liturgy of the Hours, Eucharistic adoration, *Lectio divina*, the Holy Rosary, meditation. All these expressions of prayer, which have their center in the Eucharist, fulfill the words of Jesus.

Homily at Mass for the ordination of priests
May 3, 2009

The Priestly Fraternity

64. *Priestly fraternity*

There is a need for all of us to move beyond sterile divisions, disagreements and preconceptions, and to listen together to the voice of the Spirit who is guiding the Church into a future of hope. Each of us knows how important priestly fraternity has been in our lives. That fraternity is not only a precious possession, but also an immense resource for the renewal of the priesthood and the raising up of new vocations.

> *Response to questions by the bishops of the*
> *United States in Washington, D.C.*
> *April 16, 2008*

65. *The presbyterate*

And it is therefore important to live in the reality of the presbyterate, of the community of priests who help one another, who are journeying on together with solidarity in their common faith. This also seems to me to be important, for if young people see priests who are very lonely, sad and tired, they will think: "If this is my future, then it is not for me." A real communion of life that shows young people:

"Yes, this can be a future for me too, it is possible to live like this," must be created.

Meeting with clergy of the Diocese of Aosta, Italy
July 25, 2005

66. Communion

Priests, even if they live far apart, are a true community of brothers who should support and help one another. This communion among priests is as important today as ever. In order not to drift into isolation, into loneliness with its sorrows, it is important for us to meet one another regularly.

Meeting with clergy of the
Diocese of Bolzano-Bressanone
August 6, 2008

67. Presbyterate

No priest is a priest on his own; we are a presbyterate and it is only in this communion with the Bishop that each one can carry out his service.

Meeting with clergy of the
Diocese of Bolzano-Bressanone
August 6, 2008

68. *Virtue*

[There is a need to develop virtues such as] gratitude, patience and also acceptance of the inevitable sufferings. In marriage too, there is always suffering and tension. Yet, the couple goes forward and thus true love matures. The same thing happens in the Church's communities: let us be patient together. The different levels of the hierarchy too—from the parish priest to the Bishop, to the Supreme Pontiff—must continually exchange ideas with one another, they must foster dialogue to find together the best road. The experiences of parish priests are fundamental and so are the experiences of the Bishop, and let us say, the universal perspectives of the Pope have a theological and pastoral place of their own in the Church.

> *Meeting with clergy of the Diocese of Rome*
> *February 22, 2007*

69. *The example of the bishop*

If you [bishops] yourselves live in a manner closely config-
ured to Christ, the Good Shepherd, who laid down his life
for his sheep, you will inspire your brother priests to reded-
icate themselves to the service of their flocks with Christ-
like generosity. Indeed a clearer focus upon the imitation of
Christ in holiness of life is exactly what is needed in order
for us to move forward.

Address to the bishops of the
United States in Washington, D.C.
April 16, 2008

Exemplary Figures

70. *Saint Joseph*

The example of Saint Joseph, a "just man," the Evangelist says, fully responsible before God and before Mary, should be an encouragement to all of you on your way towards the priesthood. Joseph appears to us ever attentive to the voice of the Lord, who guides the events of history, and ready to follow the instructions, ever faithful, generous and detached in service, an effective teacher of prayer and of work in the hidden life at Nazareth. I can assure you, dear Seminarians, that the further you advance with God's grace on the path of the priesthood, the more you will experience what abundant spiritual fruits result from calling on Saint Joseph and invoking his support in carrying out your daily duty.

Visit to the Roman Major Seminary
February 25, 2006

71. Saint Peter

It seems to me that throughout his time of discipleship, even until his own crucifixion, Saint Peter always had to listen anew to Jesus, to enter more profoundly into the mystery of his priesthood, of Christ's priesthood communicated to the Apostles and their successors. In this sense the figure of Peter appears to me like the image of all of us in these days.

Address at the conclusion of the annual Lenten retreat
February 16, 2008

72. Saint Augustine (1)

A little while ago I read what Saint Augustine said in Book X of his *Confessions*: "I was tempted and I now understand that it was a temptation to enclose myself in contemplative life, to seek solitude with you, O Lord; but you prevented me, you plucked me from it and made me listen to Saint Paul's words: 'Christ died for us all. Consequently, we must die with Christ and live for all.' I understood that I cannot shut myself up in contemplation; you died for us all. Therefore, with you, I must live for all and thus practice works of charity. True contemplation is expressed in works of charity. Therefore, the sign for which we have truly prayed, that we have experienced in the encounter with Christ, is that we exist 'for others.'" This is what a parish priest must be like.

Meeting with clergy of the Diocese of Rome
February 22, 2007

73. *Saint Augustine (2)*

Initially, after his conversion, [Saint] Augustine believed he had reached the summit and that he would live in the paradise of the newness of being Christian. He then discovered that life's grueling journey continued, although from that moment it was always in God's light, and that it was necessary to renew this leap out of oneself every day, necessary to give this "I" so that it might die and be renewed in the great "I" of Christ, which is in a certainly very true way the common "I" of us all, it is our "we."

> *Meeting with clergy of the Diocese of Rome*
> *February 7, 2008*

74. *The Curé d'Ars*

Every priest should be able to feel happiness in serving the Church. In the school of the Curé d'Ars, a son of your land and patron of pastors throughout the world, constantly reiterate that the greatest thing a man can do is to give the body and blood of Christ to the faithful and to forgive their sins.

> *Meeting with the bishops of France*
> *September 14, 2008*

75. Fr. Andrea Santoro

We have the shining example of Fr. Andrea, who shows us what it means to "be" a priest to the very end: dying for Christ during a moment of prayer, thereby witnessing on the one hand to the interiority of his own life with Christ, and on the other, to his own witness for people at a truly "panperipheral" point in the world, surrounded by hatred and the fanaticism of others. It is a witness that inspires everyone to follow Christ, to give one's life for others and thus to find Life.

> *Meeting with clergy of the Diocese of Rome*
> *March 2, 2006*

V. THE GOOD SHEPHERD

76. *The adventure of priesthood*

Indeed, even though it may seem that the priest's life does not attract most people's interest, it is in fact the most interesting and necessary adventure for the world, the adventure of showing, of making present, the fullness of life to which we all aspire.

Homily at Vespers in the Roman Major Seminary
February 1, 2008

Mission

77. The heart of the vocation

In his account of the call of the Twelve, [Mark] says: "Jesus appointed twelve to be with him and to be sent out" (3:14). To be with Jesus and, being sent, to go out to meet people—these two things belong together and together they are the heart of a vocation, of the priesthood. To be with him and to be sent out—the two are inseparable. Only one who is "with him" comes to know him and can truly proclaim him. And anyone who has been with him cannot keep to himself what he has found; instead, he has to pass it on.

> *Homily at Vespers with seminarians and*
> *religious in Altötting, Bavaria*
> *September 11, 2006*

78. *Pastor of souls*

A priest, a pastor of souls, must first and foremost be concerned with those who believe and live with the Church, who seek in her their way of life and on their part, like living stones, build the Church, hence, also build and support the priest. However, we must also—as the Lord says—go out ever anew "to the highways and hedges" (Lk 14:23), to deliver God's invitation to his banquet also to those who have so far heard nothing or have not been stirred within.

> *Homily at Mass for the ordination of priests*
> *May 7, 2006*

79. *Humility*

[To pray, to provide care, and to preach are] great priorities in the work of a disciple of Christ, a priest. . . . By interweaving these three priorities and, naturally, taking into account all the human aspects, including our own limitations that we must recognize, we can properly fulfill our priesthood. This humility that recognizes the limitations of our own strength is important as well. All that we cannot do, the Lord must do.

> *Meeting with clergy of the Dioceses of*
> *Belluno-Feltre and Treviso*
> *July 24, 2007*

80. *Counsel*

I think these things are essential [in the daily life of a priest]: the Eucharist, the Office of Readings, prayer and a conversation every day, even a brief one, with the Lord on his words which I must proclaim. And never lose either your friendship with priests, listening to the voice of the living Church, or naturally, availability to the people entrusted to me, because from these very people, with their suffering, their faith experiences, their doubts and difficulties, we too can learn, seek and find God, find our Lord Jesus Christ.

Visit to the Roman Major Seminary
February 17, 2007

81. *Misunderstanding*

It is true, and we priests experience this: the "world" . . . does not understand the Christian, does not understand the ministers of the Gospel. Somewhat because it does not know God, and somewhat because it does not want to know him. The world does not want to know God so as not to be disturbed by his will, and therefore it does not want to listen to his ministers; this could cause a crisis.

Homily at Mass for the ordination of priests
May 3, 2009

Proclamation

82. *The question*

The fundamental question of our pastoral work is how to bring God to the world, to our contemporaries. . . . Bringing God implies above all, on the one hand, love, and on the other, hope and faith. Thus, the dimension of life lived, bearing the best witness for Christ, the best proclamation, is always the life of true Christians.

> *Meeting with clergy of the Dioceses of*
> *Belluno-Feltre and Treviso*
> *July 24, 2007*

83. *Proclamation*

At the heart of the mission of Jesus Christ and of every Christian is the proclamation of the Kingdom of God. Proclaiming the Kingdom in the name of Christ means for the Church, for priests, men and women religious, and for all the baptized, a commitment to be present in the world as his witnesses.

> *Homily at Vespers with clergy and*
> *religious at Mariazell, Austria*
> *September 8, 2007*

84. *Duty*

Pastors themselves, first and foremost, must be preachers of the faith, leading new disciples to Christ.

> *Meeting with the bishops of Cameroon in Yaoundé*
> *March 18, 2009*

85. *Mission*

This is also your mission [as priests]: to bring the Gospel to everyone so that everyone may experience the joy of Christ and that there be joy in every city. What can be more beautiful than this? What can be greater, more exciting, than cooperating in spreading the Word of life in the world, than communicating the living water of the Holy Spirit? To proclaim and to witness joy: this is the central core of your mission.

> *Homily at Mass for the ordination of priests*
> *April 27, 2008*

86. *Service*

"To serve the Lord"—priestly service precisely also means to learn to know the Lord in his Word and to make it known to all those he entrusts to us.

> *Homily at Chrism Mass, Holy Thursday*
> *March 20, 2008*

87. *The Word*

The Word of God is not only written but, thanks to the testimonies that the Lord in the sacrament has inscribed in the apostolic ministry, it remains a living word.

Homily at Mass on the Solemnity of SS. Peter and Paul
June 29, 2005

88. *Instruments*

What marvels surround our work [of administering the divine sacraments] in the service of God's word! We are instruments of the Holy Spirit; God is so humble that he uses us to spread his word. We become his voice, once we have listened carefully to the word coming from his mouth. We place his word on our lips in order to bring it to the world.

Homily at Vespers with clergy and
religious in Lourdes, France
September 12, 2008

89. *Soul*

Even now the word of God is given to us as the soul of our apostolate, the soul of our priestly life.

Homily at Vespers with clergy and
religious in Lourdes, France
September 12, 2008

90. Fidei donum *[gift of faith]*

I see it during the *Ad limina* visits: [that] . . . priests are working, even in Papua New Guinea, the Solomon Islands and regions beyond the wildest imagination, scattering the seed of the Word, identifying with people. Thus, they imbue this threatened world, invaded by so many negative things from the West, with the great power of faith and with it, all that is positive in what we are given.

Meeting with the bishops of Germany in Cologne
August 21, 2005

Care

91. *Portrait*

The Apostle Paul's words can apply to us: "Yet preaching the Gospel is not the subject of a boast; I am under compulsion and have no choice. I am ruined if I do not preach it! . . . Although I am not bound to anyone, I made myself the slave of all so as to win over as many as possible. . . . I have made myself all things to all men in order to save at least some of them" (1 Cor 9:16-22). These words that are the self-portrait of the Apostle are also the portrait of every priest. Making oneself "all things to all men" is expressed in daily life, in attention to every person and family.

> *Address to clergy of the Diocese of Rome*
> *May 13, 2005*

92. *Priestly hope*

"Priestly hope" [is] that of Jesus the Good Shepherd who dwells within you and gives shape to your desires in accordance with his divine Heart: a hope of life and forgiveness for the people who will be entrusted to your pastoral care; a hope of holiness and apostolic fruitfulness for yourselves and for all the Church; a hope of openness to faith and to the encounter with God for those who support you in their quest for the truth; a hope of peace and comfort for the suffering and for those wounded by life.

> *Homily at Mass for the ordination of priests*
> *April 27, 2008*

93. *Practice*

It is not enough to preach or to carry out pastoral work with the precious knowledge acquired in the study of theology. This is important and fundamental but it must be assimilated: from academic knowledge, which we have learned and upon which we have reflected, within a personal vision of life, in order then to reach out to other people.

> *Meeting with clergy of the Diocese of Rome*
> *February 26, 2009*

94. *With the heart*

There is no true knowledge without love, without an inner relationship and deep acceptance of the other. The shepherd cannot be satisfied with knowing names and dates. His way of knowing his sheep must always also be knowing with the heart.

> *Homily at Mass for the ordination of priests*
> *May 7, 2006*

95. Youth (1)

We know that the young really must be a priority of our pastoral work because they dwell in a world far from God. And in our cultural context it is not easy to encounter Christ, the Christian life and the faith life.

Meeting with clergy of the Diocese of Rome
February 22, 2007

96. Youth (2)

I think that this is the fundamental point of our pastoral care for young people, for everyone but especially for the young: to draw attention to the choice of God who is life, to the fact that God exists—and he exists very concretely— and also to teach friendship with Jesus Christ.

Meeting with clergy of the Diocese of Rome
February 7, 2008

97. Youth (3)

The priest as an educator must himself have received a good training and must fit into today's culture, and be deeply cultured if he is to help young people to enter a culture inspired by faith. I would naturally add that in the end, the central point of orientation in every culture is God, God present in Christ.

Meeting with clergy of the Diocese of Rome
February 26, 2009

98. *The parish priest*

Who knows the men and women of today better than the parish priest? . . . And people often come here to the parish priest, usually openly, with no pretext other than suffering, sickness, death or family matters. And they come to the confessional stripped of any veneer, with their very being. No other "profession," it seems to me, gives this possibility of knowing the person as he is, in his humanity, rather than in the role he plays in society. In this sense, we can truly study the person in his core, beyond roles, and learn ourselves what it is to be human, what it is to be in the school of Christ. To this end, it is absolutely important to come to understand the human being, the human being of today, in ourselves and with others, but also always listening attentively to the Lord and accepting in myself the seed of the word, so that it may become leaven within me and become communicable to others.

Meeting with clergy of the Diocese of Rome
February 26, 2009

99. *The parish*

One of the tasks of the parish [is] offering hospitality to those who have no experience of normal parish life. We must not be a circle closed in on ourselves. We have our customs but still we must be open and endeavor to create "vestibules," that is, places which will draw others closer. Someone who comes from afar cannot immediately enter parish life, which already has its own practices. For such a person everything is novel, far removed from his own life. Therefore, with the help of the word, we must seek to create what the early Church created with the catechumenates: spaces in which one begins to live the word, to follow the word, to make it understandable and realistic, corresponding to forms of actual experience. In this sense I think that [it] . . . is very important, that is, the need to associate the word with the witness of a just life, being for others, opening oneself to the poor, to the needy, and also to the rich who need to have their hearts opened, to feel someone knocking at their hearts. So, it is a question of different avenues, according to the situation.

Meeting with clergy of the Diocese of Rome
February 26, 2009

100. *Oratories*

This is precisely the role of such a center, that one not only finds possibilities there for one's leisure time but above all for an integral human formation that completes the personality.

Meeting with clergy of the Diocese of Rome
February 26, 2009

101. *The relationship with the laity*

It can never be said often enough that the priesthood is indispensable to the Church, for it is at the service of the laity. Priests are a gift from God for the Church. Where their specific missions are concerned, priests cannot delegate their functions to the faithful.

Meeting with the bishops of France
September 14, 2008

The Pastoral Care of Vocations

102. *Vitality*

The ability to cultivate vocations to the priesthood and the religious life is a sure sign of the health of a local Church.

> *Response to questions by the bishops of the*
> *United States in Washington, D.C.*
> *April 16, 2008*

103. *Call*

The discernment of a vocation is above all the fruit of an intimate dialogue between the Lord and his disciples. Young people, if they know how to pray, can be trusted to know what to do with God's call.

> *Response to questions by the bishops of the*
> *United States in Washington, D.C.*
> *April 16, 2008*

104. *Witness*

The witness of a priestly life well lived brings nobility to the Church, calls forth admiration among the faithful, and is a source of blessings for the community; it is the best way to promote vocations, the most authentic invitation to other young people to respond positively to the Lord's call. It is true collaboration in building the Kingdom of God!

Meeting with clergy and religious in Aparecida, Brazil
May 12, 2007

105. *Exhortation*

I urge you [seminarians] to deepen your friendship with Jesus the Good Shepherd. Talk heart to heart with him. Reject any temptation to ostentation, careerism, or conceit. Strive for a pattern of life truly marked by charity, chastity and humility, in imitation of Christ, the Eternal High Priest, of whom you are to become living icons (cf. *I Will Give You Shepherds* [*Pastores Dabo Vobis*], no. 33). Dear seminarians, I pray for you daily. Remember that what counts before the Lord is to dwell in his love and to make his love shine forth for others.

Meeting with youth and seminarians
in Yonkers, New York
April 19, 2008

106. *The seminary*

The Seminary is a precious investment for the future, because it ensures that through patient and generous work the Christian community will not be deprived of shepherds of souls, of teachers of faith and of zealous guides and witnesses of Christ's charity.

Meeting with priests in the Cathedral of Brindisi
June 15, 2008

107. *Formation*

It is necessary to guide seminarians to a personal experience of God through personal and communal daily prayer, and above all through the Eucharist, celebrated and experienced as the center of their very existence.

Meeting with priests, seminarians, and
students in Sardinia, Italy
September 7, 2008

108. *Time*

This is what a seminary is: more than a place, it is a significant time in the life of a follower of Jesus.

Meeting with seminarians for the
Twentieth World Youth Day
August 19, 2005

109. *Falling in love*

The seminarian experiences the beauty of that call in a moment of grace which could be defined as "falling in love." His soul is filled with amazement, which makes him ask in prayer: "Lord, why me?" But love knows no "why;" it is a free gift to which one responds with the gift of self.

Meeting with seminarians for the
Twentieth World Youth Day
August 19, 2005

ENTRUSTING TO MARY

110. *Entrusting to Mary*

May the Virgin, who promptly answered the call of the Father saying, "Behold, I am the handmaid of the Lord" (Lk 1:38), intercede so that the Christian people will not lack servants of divine joy: priests who, in communion with their Bishops, announce the Gospel faithfully and celebrate the sacraments, take care of the people of God, and are ready to evangelize all humanity.

Message for the Forty-Fourth World Day of Vocations
February 10, 2007

111. *Mary, mother of priests*

Mary, the heavenly Mother of priests, . . . who beneath the Cross united herself with the Sacrifice of her Son and after the Resurrection accepted together with the other disciples the gift of the Spirit, help you and each one of us, dear brothers in the priesthood, to allow ourselves to be inwardly transformed by God's grace. Only in this way is it possible to be faithful images of the Good Shepherd; only in this way can we carry out joyfully the mission of knowing, guiding and loving the flock which Jesus acquired at the price of his blood.

> *Homily at Mass for the ordination of priests for*
> *the Diocese of Rome*
> *April 29, 2007*

112. *Disciples of Mary*

On your journey of preparation, and in your . . . priestly ministry, let Mary guide you as you "learn" Jesus. Keep your eyes fixed on him. Let him form you, so that in your ministry you will be able to show him to all who approach you. When you take into your hands the Eucharistic Body of Jesus so as to nourish his People, and when you assume responsibility for that part of the Mystical Body which will be entrusted to you, remember the attitude of wonder and adoration which characterized Mary's faith.

> *Meeting with clergy and religious at the*
> *Shrine of Jasna Góra, Poland*
> *May 26, 2006*

APPENDIX

Letter of His Holiness
Pope Benedict XVI
Proclaiming a Year for Priests
on the 150th Anniversary of
the *"Dies Natalis"*
of the Curé of Ars

Dear Brother Priests,

On the forthcoming Solemnity of the Most Sacred
Heart of Jesus, Friday, June 19, 2009—a day traditionally
devoted to prayer for the sanctification of the clergy—I have
decided to inaugurate a "Year for Priests" in celebration of
the 150th anniversary of the "*dies natalis*" of John Mary
Vianney, the patron saint of parish priests worldwide.[1]
This Year, meant to deepen the commitment of all priests
to interior renewal for the sake of a more forceful and inci-
sive witness to the Gospel in today's world, will conclude
on the same Solemnity in 2010. "The priesthood is the love

of the heart of Jesus," the saintly Curé of Ars would often say.[2] This touching expression makes us reflect, first of all, with heartfelt gratitude on the immense gift which priests represent, not only for the Church, but also for humanity itself. I think of all those priests who quietly present Christ's words and actions each day to the faithful and to the whole world, striving to be one with the Lord in their thoughts and their will, their sentiments and their style of life. How can I not pay tribute to their apostolic labors, their tireless and hidden service, their universal charity? And how can I not praise the courageous fidelity of so many priests who, even amid difficulties and incomprehension, remain faithful to their vocation as "friends of Christ," whom he has called by name, chosen and sent?

I still treasure the memory of the first parish priest at whose side I exercised my ministry as a young priest: he left me an example of unreserved devotion to his pastoral duties, even to meeting death in the act of bringing viaticum to a gravely ill person. I also recall the countless confreres whom I have met and continue to meet, not least in my pastoral visits to different countries: men generously dedicated to the daily exercise of their priestly ministry. Yet the expression of Saint John Mary also makes us think of Christ's pierced Heart and the crown of thorns which surrounds it. I am also led to think, therefore, of the countless situations of suffering endured by many priests, either because they themselves share in the manifold human experience of pain or because they encounter misunderstanding from the very persons to whom they minister. How can we not also think of all those priests who are offended in their dignity, obstructed in their mission and persecuted, even at times to offering the supreme testimony of their own blood?

There are also, sad to say, situations which can never be sufficiently deplored where the Church herself suffers as a consequence of infidelity on the part of some of her ministers. Then it is the world which finds grounds for scandal and rejection. What is most helpful to the Church in such cases is not only a frank and complete acknowledgment of the weaknesses of her ministers, but also a joyful and renewed realization of the greatness of God's gift, embodied in the splendid example of generous pastors, religious afire with love for God and for souls, and insightful, patient spiritual guides. Here the teaching and example of Saint John Mary Vianney can serve as a significant point of reference for us all. The Curé of Ars was quite humble, yet as a priest he was conscious of being an immense gift to his people: "A good shepherd, a pastor after God's heart, is the greatest treasure which the good Lord can grant to a parish, and one of the most precious gifts of divine mercy."[3] He spoke of the priesthood as if incapable of fathoming the grandeur of the *gift* and *task* entrusted to a human creature: "O, how great is the priest! . . . If he realized what he is, he would die . . . God obeys him: he utters a few words and the Lord descends from heaven at his voice, to be contained within a small host. . . ."[4] Explaining to his parishioners the importance of the sacraments, he would say: "Without the Sacrament of Holy Orders, we would not have the Lord. Who put him there in that tabernacle? The priest. Who welcomed your soul at the beginning of your life? The priest. Who feeds your soul and gives it strength for its journey? The priest. Who will prepare it to appear before God, bathing it one last time in the blood of Jesus Christ? The priest, always the priest. And if this soul should happen to die [as a result of sin], who will raise it up, who will restore its calm and peace? Again, the priest. . . . After God, the priest is everything! . . . Only in heaven will he fully realize what he is."[5] These words, welling up from the priestly heart of the holy pastor, might sound excessive. Yet they reveal the high esteem in which he held the sacrament of the priesthood. He seemed overwhelmed by a boundless sense of responsibility: "Were we to fully realize what a priest is on earth, we would die: not of fright, but of love. . . . Without the priest, the passion and death of our Lord would be of no avail. It is the priest who continues the work of redemption on earth. . . . What use would be a house filled with gold, were there no one to open its door? The priest holds the key to the treasures of heaven: it is he who opens the door: he is the steward of the good Lord; the administrator of his goods. . . . Leave a parish for twenty years without a priest, and they will end by worshiping the beasts there. . . . The priest is not a priest for himself, he is a priest for you."[6]

He arrived in Ars, a village of 230 souls, warned by his Bishop beforehand that there he would find religious practice in a sorry state: "There is little love of God in that parish; you will be the one to put it there." As a result, he was deeply aware that he needed to go there to embody Christ's presence and to bear witness to his saving mercy: "[Lord,] grant me the conversion of my parish; I am willing to suffer whatever you wish, for my entire life!": with this prayer he entered upon his mission.[7] The Curé devoted himself completely to his parish's conversion, setting before all else the Christian education of the people in his care. Dear brother priests, let us ask the Lord Jesus for the grace to learn for ourselves something of the pastoral plan of Saint John Mary Vianney! The first thing we need to learn is the complete identification of the man with his ministry. In Jesus, person and mission tend to coincide: all Christ's saving activity was, and is, an expression of his "filial consciousness" which from all eternity stands before the Father in an attitude of loving submission to his will. In a humble yet genuine way, every priest must aim for a similar identification. Certainly this is not to forget that the efficacy of the ministry is independent of the holiness of the minister; but neither can we overlook the extraordinary fruitfulness of the encounter between the ministry's objective holiness and the subjective holiness of the minister. The Curé of Ars immediately set about this patient and humble task of harmonizing his life as a minister with the holiness of the ministry he had received, by deciding to "*live*," physically, in his parish church: as his first biographer tells us: "Upon his arrival, he chose the church as his home. He entered the church before dawn and did not leave it until after the evening Angelus. There he was to be sought whenever needed."[8]

The pious excess of his devout biographer should not blind us to the fact that the Curé also knew how to "live" actively within the entire territory of his parish: he regularly visited the sick and families, organized popular missions and patronal feasts, collected and managed funds for his charitable and missionary works, embellished and furnished his parish church, cared for the orphans and teachers of the "*Providence*" (an institute he founded); provided for the education of children; founded confraternities and enlisted lay persons to work at his side.

His example naturally leads me to point out that there are sectors of cooperation which need to be opened ever more fully to the lay faithful. Priests and laity together make up the one priestly people,[9] and in virtue of their ministry priests live in the midst of the lay faithful, "that they may lead everyone to the unity of charity, 'loving one another with mutual affection; and outdoing one another in sharing honor'" (Rom 12:10).[10] Here we ought to recall the Second Vatican Council's hearty encouragement to priests "to be sincere in their appreciation and promotion of the dignity of the laity and of the special role they have to play in the Church's mission. . . . They should be willing to listen to lay people, give brotherly consideration to their wishes, and acknowledge their experience and competence in the different fields of human activity. In this way they will be able together with them to discern the signs of the times."[11]

Saint John Mary Vianney taught his parishioners primarily by the witness of his life. It was from his example that they learned to pray, halting frequently before the tabernacle for a visit to Jesus in the Blessed Sacrament.[12] "One need not say much to pray well"—the Curé explained to them— "We know that Jesus is there in the tabernacle: let us open our hearts to him, let us rejoice in his sacred presence. That is the best prayer."[13] And he would urge them: "Come to communion, my brothers and sisters, come to Jesus. Come to live from him in order to live with him. . . ."[14] "Of course you are not worthy of him, but *you need him!*"[15] This way of educating the faithful *to the Eucharistic presence and to communion* proved most effective when they saw him celebrate the Holy Sacrifice of the Mass. Those present said that "it was not possible to find a finer example of worship. . . . He gazed upon the Host with immense love."[16] "All good works, taken together, do not equal the sacrifice of the Mass"—he would say—"since they are human works, while the Holy Mass is the work of God."[17] He was convinced that the fervor of a priest's life depended entirely upon the Mass: "The reason why a priest is lax is that he does not pay attention to the Mass! My God, how we ought to pity a priest who celebrates as if he were engaged in something routine!"[18] He was accustomed, when celebrating, also to offer his own life in sacrifice: "What a good thing it is for a priest each morning to offer himself to God in sacrifice!"[19]

This deep personal identification with the Sacrifice of the Cross led him—by a sole inward movement—from the altar to the confessional. Priests ought never to be resigned to empty confessionals or the apparent indifference of the faithful to this sacrament. In France, at the time of the Curé of Ars, confession was no more easy or frequent than in our own day, since the upheaval caused by the revolution had long inhibited the practice of religion. Yet he sought in every way, by his preaching and his powers of persuasion, to help his parishioners to rediscover the meaning and beauty of the sacrament of Penance, presenting it as an inherent demand of the Eucharistic presence. He thus created a *"virtuous"* circle. By spending long hours in church before the tabernacle, he inspired the faithful to imitate him by coming to visit Jesus with the knowledge that their parish priest would be there, ready to listen and offer forgiveness. Later, the growing numbers of penitents from all over France would keep him in the confessional for up to sixteen hours a day. It was said that Ars had become "a great hospital of souls."[20] His first biographer relates that "the grace he obtained [for the conversion of sinners] was so powerful that it would pursue them, not leaving them a moment of peace!"[21] The saintly Curé reflected something of the same idea when he said: "It is not the sinner who returns to God to beg his forgiveness, but God himself who runs after the sinner and makes him return to him."[22] "This good Savior is so filled with love that he seeks us everywhere."[23]

We priests should feel that the following words, which he put on the lips of Christ, are meant for each of us personally: "I will charge my ministers to proclaim to sinners that I am ever ready to welcome them, that my mercy is infinite."[24] From Saint John Mary Vianney we can learn to put our unfailing trust in the sacrament of Penance, to set it once more at the center of our pastoral concerns, and to take up the "dialogue of salvation" which it entails. The Curé of Ars dealt with different penitents in different ways. Those who came to his confessional drawn by a deep and humble longing for God's forgiveness found in him the encouragement to plunge into the "flood of divine mercy" which sweeps everything away by its vehemence. If someone was troubled by the thought of his own frailty and inconstancy, and fearful of sinning again, the Curé would unveil the mystery of God's love in these beautiful and touching words: "The good Lord knows everything.

Even before you confess, he already knows that you will sin again, yet he still forgives you. How great is the love of our God: he *even forces himself to forget the future*, so that he can grant us his forgiveness!"[25] But to those who made a lukewarm and rather indifferent confession of sin, he clearly demonstrated by his own tears of pain how "abominable" this attitude was: "I weep because you don't weep,"[26] he would say. "If only the Lord were not so good! *But he is so good!* One would have to be a brute to treat so good a Father this way!"[27] He awakened repentance in the hearts of the lukewarm by forcing them to see God's own pain at their sins reflected in the face of the priest who was their confessor. To those who, on the other hand, came to him already desirous of and suited to a deeper spiritual life, he flung open the abyss of God's love, explaining the untold beauty of living in union with him and dwelling in his presence: "Everything in God's sight, everything with God, everything to please God. . . . How beautiful it is!"[28] And he taught them to pray: "My God, grant me the grace to love you as much as I possibly can."[29]

In his time the Curé of Ars was able to transform the hearts and the lives of so many people because he enabled them to experience the Lord's merciful love. Our own time urgently needs a similar proclamation and witness to the truth of Love: *Deus caritas est* (1 Jn 4:8). Thanks to the word and the sacraments of Jesus, John Mary Vianney built up his flock, although he often trembled from a conviction of his personal inadequacy, and desired more than once to withdraw from the responsibilities of the parish ministry out of a sense of his unworthiness. Nonetheless, with exemplary obedience he never abandoned his post, consumed as he was by apostolic zeal for the salvation of souls. He sought to remain completely faithful to his own vocation and mission through the practice of an austere asceticism: "The great misfortune for us parish priests"—he lamented—"is that our souls grow tepid"; meaning by this that a pastor can grow dangerously inured to the state of sin or of indifference in which so many of his flock are living.[30] He himself kept a tight rein on his body, with vigils and fasts, lest it rebel against·his priestly soul. Nor did he avoid self-mortification for the good of the souls in his care and as a help to expiating the many sins he heard in confession. To a priestly confrere he explained: "I will tell you my recipe: I give sinners a small penance and the rest I do in their place."[31] Aside from the actual penances which the Curé of Ars practiced, the core of his teaching remains valid for each of us: souls have been won at the price of Jesus' own blood, and a priest cannot devote himself to their salvation if he refuses to share personally in the "precious cost" of redemption.

In today's world, as in the troubled times of the Curé of Ars, the lives and activity of priests need to be distinguished by *a forceful witness to the Gospel*. As Pope Paul VI rightly noted, "modern man listens more willingly to witnesses than to teachers, and if he does listen to teachers, it is because they are witnesses."[32] Lest we experience existential emptiness and the effectiveness of our ministry be compromised, we need to ask ourselves ever anew: "Are we truly pervaded by the word of God? Is that word truly the nourishment we live by, even more than bread and the things of this world? Do we really know that word? Do we love it? Are we deeply engaged with this word to the point that it really leaves a mark on our lives and shapes our thinking?"[33] Just as Jesus called the Twelve to be with him (cf. Mk 3:14), and only later sent them forth to preach, so too in our days priests are called to assimilate that "new style of life" which was inaugurated by the Lord Jesus and taken up by the Apostles.[34]

It was complete commitment to this "new style of life" which marked the priestly ministry of the Curé of Ars. Pope John XXIII, in his Encyclical Letter *Sacerdotii nostri primordia*, published in 1959 on the first centenary of the death of Saint John Mary Vianney, presented his asceticism with special reference to the "three evangelical counsels" which the Pope considered necessary also for priests: "even though priests are not bound to embrace these evangelical counsels by virtue of the clerical state, these counsels nonetheless offer them, as they do all the faithful, the surest road to the desired goal of Christian perfection."[35] The Curé of Ars lived the "evangelical counsels" in a way suited to his priestly state. His *poverty* was not the poverty of a religious or a monk, but that proper to a priest: while managing much money (since well-to-do pilgrims naturally took an interest in his charitable works), he realized that everything had been donated to his church, his poor, his orphans, the girls of his "*Providence*,"[36] his families of modest means. Consequently, he "was rich in giving to others and very poor for himself."[37] As he would explain: "My secret is simple: give everything away; hold nothing back."[38] When he lacked money, he would say amiably to the poor who knocked at his door: "Today I'm poor just like you, I'm one of you."[39] At the end of his life, he could say with absolute tranquility: "I no longer have anything. The good Lord can call me whenever he wants!"[40] His *chastity*, too, was that demanded of a priest for his ministry. It could be said that it was a chastity suited to one who must daily touch the Eucharist, who contemplates it blissfully and with that same bliss offers it to his flock. It was said of him that "he radiated chastity"; the faithful would see this when he turned and gazed at the tabernacle with loving eyes."[41] Finally, Saint John Mary Vianney's *obedience* found full embodiment in his conscientious fidelity to the daily demands of his ministry. We know how he was tormented by the thought of his inadequacy for parish ministry and by a desire to flee "in order to bewail his poor life, in solitude."[42] Only obedience and a thirst for souls convinced him to remain at his post. As he explained to himself and his flock: "There are no two good ways of serving God. There is only one: serve him as he desires to be served."[43] He considered this the golden rule for a life of obedience: "Do only what can be offered to the good Lord."[44]

In this context of a spirituality nourished by the practice of the evangelical counsels, I would like to invite all priests, during this Year dedicated to them, to welcome the new springtime which the Spirit is now bringing about in the Church, not least through the ecclesial movements and the new communities. "In his gifts the Spirit is multifaceted. . . . He breathes where he wills. He does so unexpectedly, in unexpected places, and in ways previously unheard of . . . but he also shows us that he works with a view to the one body and in the unity of the one body."[45] In this regard, the statement of the Decree *Presbyterorum Ordinis* continues to be timely: "While testing the spirits to discover if they be of God, priests must discover with faith, recognize with joy and foster diligently the many and varied charismatic gifts of the laity, whether these be of a humble or more exalted kind."[46] These gifts, which awaken in many people the desire for a deeper spiritual life, can benefit not only the lay faithful but the clergy as well. The communion between ordained and charismatic ministries can provide "a helpful impulse to a renewed commitment by the Church in proclaiming and bearing witness to the Gospel of hope and charity in every corner of the world."[47] I would also like to add, echoing the Apostolic Exhortation *Pastores Dabo Vobis* of Pope John Paul II, that the ordained ministry has a radical "*communitarian form*" and can be exercised only in the communion of priests with their Bishop.[48] This communion between priests and their Bishop, grounded in the sacrament of Holy Orders and made manifest in Eucharistic concelebration, needs to be translated into various concrete expressions of an effective and affective priestly fraternity.[49] Only thus will priests be able to live fully the gift of celibacy and build thriving Christian communities in which the miracles which accompanied the first preaching of the Gospel can be repeated.

The Pauline Year now coming to its close invites us also to look to the Apostle of the Gentiles, who represents a splendid example of a priest entirely devoted to his ministry. "The love of Christ urges us on"—he wrote—"because we are convinced that one has died for all; therefore all have died" (2 Cor 5:14). And he adds: "He died for all, so that those who live might live no longer for themselves, but for him who died and was raised for them" (2 Cor 5:15). Could a finer program be proposed to any priest resolved to advance along the path of Christian perfection?

Dear brother priests, the celebration of the 150th anniversary of the death of Saint John Mary Vianney (1859) follows upon the celebration of the 150th anniversary of the apparitions of Lourdes (1858). In 1959 Blessed Pope John XXIII noted that "shortly before the Curé of Ars completed his long and admirable life, the Immaculate Virgin appeared in another part of France to an innocent and humble girl, and entrusted to her a message of prayer and penance which continues, even a century later, to yield immense spiritual fruits. The life of this holy priest whose centenary we are commemorating in a real way anticipated the great supernatural truths taught to the seer of Massabielle. He was greatly devoted to the Immaculate Conception of the Blessed Virgin; in 1836 he had dedicated his parish church to Our Lady Conceived without Sin and he greeted the dogmatic definition of this truth in 1854 with deep faith and great joy."[50] The Curé would always remind his faithful that "after giving us all he could, Jesus Christ wishes in addition to bequeath us his most precious possession, his Blessed Mother."[51]

To the Most Holy Virgin I entrust this Year for Priests. I ask her to awaken in the heart of every priest a generous and renewed commitment to the ideal of complete self-oblation to Christ and the Church which inspired the thoughts and actions of the saintly Curé of Ars. It was his fervent prayer life and his impassioned love of Christ Crucified that enabled John Mary Vianney to grow daily in his total self-oblation to God and the Church. May his example lead all priests to offer that witness of unity with their Bishop, with one another and with the lay faithful, which today, as ever, is so necessary. Despite all the evil present in our world, the words which Christ spoke to his Apostles in the Upper Room continue to inspire us: "In the world you have tribulation; but take courage, I have overcome the world" (Jn 16:33). Our faith in the Divine Master gives us the strength to look to the future with confidence. Dear priests, Christ is counting on you. In the footsteps of the Curé of Ars, let yourselves be enthralled by him. In this way you too will be, for the world in our time, heralds of hope, reconciliation and peace!

With my blessing.

From the Vatican, June 16, 2009.

BENEDICTVS PP. XVI

Notes

1   He was proclaimed as such by Pope Pius XI in 1929.
2   *"Le Sacerdoce, c'est l'amour du cœur de Jésus"* (in *Le curé d'Ars. Sa pensée—Son cœur.* Présentés par l'Abbé Bernard Nodet, éd. Xavier Mappus, Foi Vivante, 1966, p. 98). Hereafter: NODET. The expression is also quoted in the *Catechism of the Catholic Church*, no. 1589.
3   NODET, p. 101.
4   Ibid., p. 97.

5   Ibid., pp. 98-99.

6   Ibid., pp. 98-100.

7   Ibid., p. 183.

8   Monnin, A., *Il Curato d'Ars. Vita di Gian.Battista-Maria Vianney*, vol. I, ed. Marietti, Turin, 1870, p. 122.

9   Cf. *Lumen Gentium*, no. 10.

10 *Presbyterorum Ordinis*, no. 9.

11 Ibid.

12 "Contemplation is a gaze of faith, fixed on Jesus. 'I look at him and he looks at me': this is what a certain peasant of Ars used to say to his holy Curé about his prayer before the tabernacle" (*Catechism of the Catholic Church*, no. 2715).

13 NODET, p. 85.

14 Ibid., p. 114.

15 Ibid., p. 119.

16 Monnin, A., op. cit., II, pp. 430ff.

17 NODET, p. 105.

18 Ibid.

19 Ibid., p. 104.

20 Monnin, A., op. cit., II, p. 293.

21 Ibid., II, p. 10.

22 NODET, p. 128.

23 Ibid., p. 50.

24 Ibid., p. 131.

25 Ibid., p. 130.

26 Ibid., p. 27.

27 Ibid., p. 139.

28 Ibid., p. 28.

29 Ibid., p. 77.

30 Ibid., p. 102.

31 Ibid., p. 189.

32 *Evangelii nuntiandi*, no. 41.

33 Benedict XVI, *Homily at the Chrism Mass*, April 9, 2009.

34 Cf. Benedict XVI, *Address to the Plenary Assembly of the Congregation for the Clergy*, March 16, 2009.

35 P. I.

37 The name given to the house where more than sixty abandoned girls were taken in and educated. To maintain this house he would do anything: "*J'ai fait tous les commerces imaginables*," he would say with a smile (NODET, p. 214).

37 NODET, p. 216.

38 Ibid., p. 215.

39 Ibid., p. 216.

40 Ibid., p. 214.

41 Cf. ibid., p. 112.

42 Cf. ibid., pp. 82-84; 102-103.

43 Ibid., p. 75.

44 Ibid., p. 76.

45 Benedict XVI, *Homily for the Vigil of Pentecost*, June 3, 2006.

46 No. 9.

47 Benedict XVI, *Address to Bishop-Friends of the Focolare Movement and the Sant'Egidio Community*, February 8, 2007.

48 Cf. No. 17.

49 Cf. John Paul II, Apostolic Exhortation *Pastores Dabo Vobis*, no. 74.

50 Encyclical Letter *Sacerdotii nostri primordia*, P. III.

51 NODET, p. 244.

INDEX

*(Numbering refers to the sequential
positioning of each thought.)*

"I am," 4, 14
    incarnation of, 3
    in relationship with, 5-6, 10
    rooted in, 8
    truth, 19
Joy: 85
Laity: 101
Lectio divina: 63
Liturgy of the Hours: 63
Love: 82, 94
Mary: 110-112
Obedience: 53
Oratory: 100
Ordinands: 21
Parishes: 99
Parish priests: 98
Poverty: 51
Prayer: 45, 55-63, 79-80
Presbyterate: 65-67
Priest:
    celibacy of, 23
    fidei donum, 90
    "I" of, 4
    mission of, 77-78, 85
    pastoral activity of, 41-42
    service of, 13, 20, 22, 48, 50, 79, 86, 91
    spiritual life of, 37-38, 41-42
    virtue of, 43-46, 68
Priesthood: 11, 14, 18, 24, 36, 76
Priestly fraternity: 64

OTHER TITLES *in the Spiritual Thoughts Series*

Pope Benedict XVI offers inspiration and encouragement through this collection of titles in the Spiritual Thoughts Series.

Family
No. 7-075, 107 pp.

The Word of God
No. 7-065, 100 pp.

St. Paul
No. 7-053, 128 pp.

Mary
No. 7-054, 172 pp.

The Saints
No. 7-055, 164 pp.

To order these resources or to obtain a catalog of other USCCB titles, visit *www.usccbpublishing.org* or call toll-free 800-235-8722. In the Washington metropolitan area or from outside the United States, call 202-722-8716. Para pedidos en español, llame al 800-235-8722 y presione 4 para hablar con un representante del servicio al cliente en español.